HAL•LEONARD®
VIOLIN PLAY-ALONG

AUDIO ACCESS INCLUDED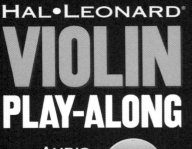

LOVE Songs

T0081793

PLAYBACK+
Speed • Pitch • Balance • Loop

To access audio visit:
www.halleonard.com/mylibrary

Enter Code
1674-7137-8248-1246

ISBN 978-1-4950-8571-0

Jon Vriesacker, violin
Audio arrangements by Peter Deneff
Recorded and Produced by Jake Johnson
at Paradyme Productions

7777 W. BLUEMOUND RD. P.O. BOX 3819 MILWAUKEE, WI 53213

Visit Hal Leonard Online at
www.halleonard.com

Can't Help Falling in Love

from the Paramount Picture BLUE HAWAII
Words and Music by George David Weiss, Hugo Peretti and Luigi Creatore

Fields of Gold

Music and Lyrics by Sting

Hey There Delilah

Words and Music by Tom Higgenson

Longer

Words and Music by Dan Fogelberg

My Heart Will Go On
(Love Theme from 'Titanic')

from the Paramount and Twentieth Century Fox Motion Picture TITANIC

Music by James Horner
Lyric by Will Jennings

Wonderful Tonight

Words and Music by Eric Clapton

Your Song

Words and Music by Elton John and Bernie Taupin

You Are So Beautiful

Words and Music by Billy Preston and Bruce Fisher